In the classroom or at home, the complete guide for using
The JGuy's Guide: The GPS for Jewish Teen Guys
by Rabbi Joseph B. Meszler, Dr. Shulamit Reinharz, Liz Suneby and Diane Heiman.

THE JGUY'S
Teacher's and Parent's
GUIDE

Rabbi Joseph B. Meszler

Co-author, *The JGuy's Guide: The GPS for Jewish Teen Guys*; author,
A Man's Responsibility: A Jewish Guide to Being a Son, a Partner in Marriage, a Father and a Community Leader

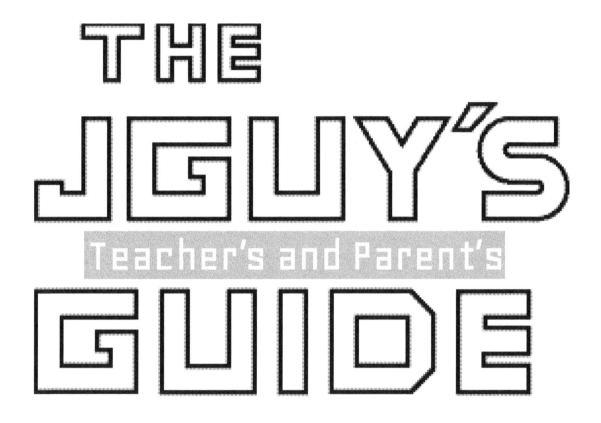

THE JGUY'S
Teacher's and Parent's
GUIDE

Rabbi Joseph B. Meszler

JEWISH LIGHTS Publishing

The JGuy's Teacher's and Parent's Guide

2013 Paperback Edition, First Printing
© 2013 by Joseph B. Meszler

Cover Design: Tim Holtz
Interior Design: Tim Holtz

For People of All Faiths, All Backgrounds
Published by Jewish Lights Publishing
www.jewishlights.com

CONTENTS

Introduction
Why *The JGuy's Guide?*

In 2008, Sylvia Barack Fishman, PhD, and Daniel Parmer, MA, of Brandeis University published research that verified what many rabbis and Jewish professionals had known for years: Jewish men were opting out of Jewish life. As a rabbi in a Reform congregation, I had noticed that women were outnumbering men at prayer services and adult education, and often girls would continue participating in Jewish religious and community life after their bat mitzvah when boys would not. My subjective experience was proven true by Fishman and Parmer:

> [Today,] Jewish men have measurably lower rates of ethnic and religious social capital than Jewish women, as characterized by involvement with distinctively Jewish activities and connections with Jewish social networks....
>
> Jewish women are more likely than Jewish men to say the religion of Judaism is "very important" to them....
>
> Liberal synagogues and temples have become "the world of our mothers"....
>
> Jewish girls and women attend synagogues more often than Jewish boys and men, especially in Reform and other liberal congregations....
>
> Jewish women are more likely than Jewish men to have visited Israel, and ranked support of Israel more highly as an important Jewish value.[1]
>
> The complex reasons behind this shift are part of the Western culture in which Jews find themselves today. In America, women tend to put a higher value on religion than men do.[2] In any case, the problem is not "matrilineal ascent," but "patrilineal descent."[3]

But there are ways to address this gender imbalance in Jewish life today. Fishman and Parmer also found that:

> Jewish men who feel strongly connected to Jews and Judaism often talk about strong male role models when they were growing up.... These role models are often recalled in "male-only" settings, whether religious (synagogues) or secular (card games, etc.)....
>
> Boys and men—like girls and women—benefit from and enjoy having gender-peer activities. These activities can help bond them to each other as Jewish males, to Jewish peoplehood now and historically, and also to Judaism culturally and religiously. Programs for Jewish boys and men are needed that create positive connections to

Jews and Jewishness, beginning with the pre-school years, targeting the all-important middle-school and teen years, and extending over the life cycle of the individual….

Synagogues and Jewish communal organizations need to find ways to balance the moral principles of egalitarianism with the psycho-social needs of boys and men to spending meaningful time in gendered peer groups.[4]

This book is a response to the reality of gender imbalance in Jewish life today. The authors of The JGuy's Guide: The GPS for Jewish Teen Guys believe that Jewish teenage guys need Jewish male role models. We also believe that there is a place for same-gender activities in egalitarian spaces because, just like women, men will talk about things differently with only men in the room. Just as there are women's seders, Rosh Hodesh women's groups, and Sisterhoods, there needs to be equally vibrant groups for boys and men.

Male-only space in a synagogue or other Jewish communal institution must look different than it used to. It cannot be based upon hierarchical power or authority. It needs to be founded on exploring what it means to be a Jewish man informed by Jewish experience and wisdom.

And let's face it: guys just want to have fun, too! This teacher's and parent's guide has fun warm-up activities and invites groups of Jewish guys in their teen years to create a safe space for personal sharing and learning. Starting with funny and ridiculous ice-breaking activities, it allows Jewish teenage guys to get to know each other before they talk about important topics like courage, bullying, speaking up, frustration, parents, God, spirituality, stress, sex, social action, and character. It presents Jewish sources in a sophisticated way; this is not a dumbed-down Jewish book.

Perhaps most important, this book includes quotes from interviews with dozens of Jewish teen guys. By engaging the perspectives of their peers, Jewish guys who read this book will feel validated. They will also have their curiosity stimulated and their assumptions challenged.

This book, therefore, answers a two-fold need. First, it provides an option for post-bar mitzvah involvement in Jewish life. In order to retain Jews after the big party, the Jewish community needs to offer a wide array of options that are flexible in time and place to be able to keep Jewish teens involved. Adolescent development deserves a Jewish voice, and this is one way to provide it.

Second, Jewish boys need Jewish male role models. It is the assumption of The JGuy's Guide and this educator's guide that a Jewish man is going to be taking the lead facilitating these activities and discussions. These chapters will give you some of what you need to talk about. Use it as a tool to eventually speak from the heart and tie yourself more deeply to your Jewish spiritual path. You will be helping yourself, the next generation, and the Jewish people.

Good luck!

Planning a Lesson

עֲשֵׂה לְךָ רַב, וּקְנֵה לְךָ חָבֵר, וֶהֱוֵי דָן אֶת כָּל הָאָדָם לְכַף זְכוּת

*Aseih l'cha rav, uk'nei l'cha chaver,
vehevei dan et kol ha'adam l'chaf z'chut.*

Get yourself a teacher, find yourself a
friend, and judge everyone favorably.
—*Pirkei Avot 1:6*

Goals

The overall goals of this book are:

- To create a safe space for teenage guys to talk personally to Jewish men who are role models and to each other.

- To bring up topics important to adolescent development for discussion among teenage guys.

- To provide sophisticated Jewish content that helps provide guidance on issues of adolescence.

Each chapter will also have its individualized goals related to its topic.

Use this guide to plan your lessons but note that one of the main features of *The JGuy's Guide* is that it is flexible. Skip around to play to your strengths as to what you are comfortable leading. There is enough material in each chapter for two or three hour-long lessons. If you are only going to do one lesson per chapter, select what you want to do and plan accordingly.

If a teenage guy opens up and starts talking and therefore you don't get to the rest of the chapter, that is fine! This book is a tool to reach the aforementioned goals. If you have reached the goals but only read one section of the book, terrific! Flexibility is key.

Warm-Up for Groups

In order for guys to get to know and feel comfortable around each other, a physical activity can serve to break down barriers. While each chapter has its own suggested physical activity, you may want to simply shoot a basketball (if inside, use a miniature, plastic indoor basketball and hoop), have a quick round-robin thumb wrestling tournament, or something similar. The activity needs to be short. Even having one guy lead the others in jumping jacks is a fun (and funny) way of getting started.

Each chapter of *The JGuy's Guide* begins with a graphic page that is designed to echo the feeling of the Talmud: a variety of ideas from many points of view. Perhaps you would like to have students look at the page together and pick a word or phrase that jumps out at them.

Finally, watching a video, listening to a song, or looking at a photograph, picture, or comic strip are great ways to trigger a discussion. Use your resources, keep them appropriate, and also keep them short. As different web addresses go in and out of use, no Internet links are published here, but in an age where everyone looks at screens, videos are an essential part of teaching.

Personal Storytelling: My Introduction and Yours

One of the essential goals of these discussions is to get teenage guys to open up and talk to Jewish men who can be role models for them. You are that guy!

They also need to feel safe talking to each other. It is critical that you create safe space in doing this personal storytelling. A simple roll of the eyes or a giggle can destroy feelings of safety. You will want to lay out these ground rules right from the start:

a) What they share is confidential to the group, not to be shared with anyone else unless the person who spoke chooses to share

b) No one may bring up anything that was said unless the person who said it brings it up first

c) Our job is to listen to each other. No one needs to fix, set straight, or give advice to anyone else.

You will have to repeat these rules with every lesson.

Safe space and personal sharing must be role modeled. In order for them to do this, you are going to have to take the plunge first! You can do this one of three ways:

a) Read the introduction to the chapter in *The JGuy's Guide* aloud, either by yourself or going around the group, each guy reading a paragraph, and then go right to the "Find Yourself a Friend" activity

b) Read the introduction aloud as a whole or in part and then add your own relevant story

c) Skip the introduction to the chapter in the book altogether and share your own story instead. Then go to the "Find Yourself a Friend" section.

If you share a story from your life, it should be personal but not too personal. You want to let students know you are a human being, but you do not want to overshare and be inappropriate. **As a general rule, you should not tell them about your sex life, anything you did under the influence of drugs or alcohol, or any kind of abuse that you suffered.** Share appropriate stories of how you have struggled and grown, how you continue to do so, who your role models have been, and what you have learned.

Find Yourself a Friend

Ask students to read through the quotations from Jewish teenage guys in each chapter in the book. Have them put a ✔ next to quotations they strongly agree with, an ✘ next to quotes they strongly disagree with, and ignore any in between. Have the guys share their ✔'s and ✘'s, and ask them why.

Select Something to Study: Did You Know?, Get Yourself a Teacher, and/or Learn

Depending on how much time you have, you may have to pick through the "Did You Know?," "Get Yourself a Teacher," or "Learn" sections and study only portions. *The JGuy's Guide* gives you an abundance of material from which to choose. If you are using a chapter for more than one lesson, perhaps you would like to use "Did You Know?" and "Get Yourself a Teacher" sections for one lesson and the "Learn" section for another lesson.

Did You Know?

For the "Did You Know?" section, have students take turns reading the facts aloud. You can ask these questions relatively consistently:

- Was there something here you already knew?

- Was there something here you didn't know or that surprised you?

- What is something you would like to know more about?

- What other facts do you know about this subject?

Get Yourself a Teacher

For the "Get Yourself a Teacher" section, you can ask the following guide questions relatively consistently:

- Did you know about this man before? If you did, is this story surprising to you?

- Describe what the man struggled with in his life. Can you relate it to something similar in your life?

- How did the man overcome or meet his struggle?

- What can you learn from him?

For the "Learn" section, the book has guide questions, and each chapter here will provide possible answers.

Journaling Time: What Do I Think?

Give students quiet time to journal in the spaces provided in the book. If you are doing this with a group, let them know you will be reading these journals privately, and you will not share anything that is written with the group. Some guys will share something more intimate in writing to you than they would ever say aloud. Respect their privacy.

Bring the lesson to a close by reading the "Text Connection" aloud, in Hebrew and English, or just in English. These are words to remember. Invite students to write them into their mobile phones as a note, or even create a photo and put them into their "lock screen" so they see them when they turn on their phones. If you are a parent, you may want to write them on a piece of paper and put them on the refrigerator as a reminder of the lesson.

If time allows, perhaps perform some kind of ritual together. For instance, if this lesson takes place before Rosh Hashanah, blow the shofar. If it takes place during Hanukkah, light Hanukkah candles. You may want to schedule lessons to coincide with different holidays in order to be able to add these rituals into the close of your lessons.

Finally, another option for closing the lesson is to share the "Text Connection" and then repeat the warm-up activity. It may feel different the second time around as students have built up trust with each other.

Courage
I Might Be Braver Than I Think

Goals

- ✡ To give guys a safe space to discuss their fears with a Jewish male role model and with each other
- ✡ To appreciate the attribute of courage and notice how it arises in our lives and in the world
- ✡ To recognize the cost of giving into fears
- ✡ To understand the value of courage from Jewish experience

Hebrew Vocabulary

חֲזַק וֶאֱמָץ

Chazak ve'ematz!

Be strong and courageous!
—Deuteronomy 31:7

Warm-up for Groups

Just participating in this group is an act of courage! As the first lesson, guys will have to get to know each other. This activity is called "Taking a First Step."

Have all of the guys take off one shoe and put it in a pile in the center of the room. Then have each guy take a shoe that is not his own. Have him find the person to whom the shoe belongs. Once he has found that person, have the person tell him his name and something new he is doing this year. The person who has his shoe will have to introduce him to the group and explain the new thing the person is doing. As each person shares, have him return the shoe he took. Go around the room and have everyone "take a first step" until all the shoes are returned. Invite students to take their seats.

Your Personal Story

Follow one of the three options explained under "Planning a Lesson."

Find Yourself a Friend

Ask students to read through the quotations from Jewish teenage guys in the book (pp. 4–6). Have them put a ✔ next to quotations they strongly agree with, an ✘ next to quotes they strongly disagree with, and ignore any in between. Have the guys share their ✔'s and ✘'s, and ask them why.

Select Something to Study: Did You Know?, Get Yourself a Teacher, and/or Learn

For "Did You Know?" and "Get Yourself a Teacher," see the relevant questions under "Planning a Lesson."

Joshua Has Big Shoes to Fill

 How do you think Joshua felt when he took over?

Teacher's tip: Joshua is clearly terrified, or else Moses would not keep repeating encouragement to him. Wouldn't you be?

How What are the main points of Moses's "pep talk" to Joshua?

Teacher's tip: Joshua should "be strong and courageous," he is in charge of dividing up the land to the Israelites and has the power to be in charge. He should be reassured and encouraged to know God is with him.

Have you ever prayed to God for courage? Do you know others who might have done so? What did they pray for?

Teacher's tip: If we pray to God to magically fix something or make something difficult go away, we usually will be disappointed. But saying a prayer before facing a challenge can help us act calmly and deliberately.

Do you think it is right to pray only when you need something?

Teacher's tip: There are many reasons to pray besides "Please help!" although that is a good reason. We can also pray to say "thank you," or "wow, this is amazing."

Out of the Dark Woods

What was Israel ben Eliezer's father trying to teach him by taking him into the woods?

Teacher's tip: Eventually everyone feels lost, alone, or abandoned, but no one is really alone.

Why did the parents eventually let their children go to school?

Teacher's tip: They were able to have trust in Israel.

Who has taught you about courage? How did they do that?

Teacher's tip: Answers can include either older role models or peers.

Have your parents ever kept you from doing something because they were afraid? Were they right or wrong to do so?

Teacher's tip: Parents act out of legitimate fear all the time. Sometimes they are "right" and sometimes they are "wrong," but they are trying to be cautious.

 Israel ben Eliezer taught the children to sing so they would not be afraid. What do you do when you are scared? How do you calm yourself down to face your fears?

Teacher's tip: Singing, playing an instrument, or simply taking a few deep breaths are great ways to face something difficult. We can also talk about our fears with people we trust.

Journaling Time: What Do I Think?

Give students quiet time to journal in the spaces provided in the book. If you are doing this with a group, remind them you will be reading these journals privately, and you will not share anything that is written with the group. Respect privacy.

Close the Lesson: Text Connection and Possible Activity

Choose one of the options explained under "Planning a Lesson."

Frenemies
I Like My Friends, but Not Always What They Do

Goals

- To compare and contrast the feeling of "frenemies"—so-called friends who can be cruel or bullies—with friends who are "brothers"—people who we trust and depend upon
- To showcase Jewish role models who stand up to bullying
- To understand the concept of *brit* (pact) as a dynamic pact of friendship

Hebrew Vocabulary

וַיִּכְרֹת יְהוֹנָתָן וְדָוִד בְּרִית

Vayichrot Yonatan v'David b'rit.

Jonathan and David sealed a pact.
—1 Samuel 18:3

בְּרִית
Brit
Covenant, pact, deep friendship

Warm-up for Groups

When they were little, your students probably played musical chairs. They also probably got hurt doing it! In this version, everyone gathers together to form a circle, with each person facing the back of the person in front of him. Have everyone slide in very close to each other. Simultaneously, have them sit down. If they do it together, they will be able to support one another in a giant "circle-sit."

An alternative warm-up activity is for the guys to create a human pyramid. Depending upon the size of the group, you can divide the guys into two teams and see which group can make a pyramid first. Everyone in the group must be included in a pyramid.

Your Personal Story

Follow one of the three options explained under "Planning a Lesson."

Find Yourself a Friend

Ask students to read through the quotations from Jewish teenage guys in the book (pp. 21–23). Have them put a ✔ next to quotations they strongly agree with, an ✘ next to quotes they strongly disagree with, and ignore any in between. Have the guys share their ✔'s and ✘'s, and ask them why.

Select Something to Study: Did You Know?, Get Yourself a Teacher, and/or Learn

For "Did You Know?" and "Get Yourself a Teacher," see the relevant questions under "Planning a Lesson."

Blood Brothers

⭐ Why do you think men who are on the same team—whether it be debate, drama, sports, or something else—bond with each other?

Teacher's tip: Learning that we need each other brings us together. Depending upon each other brings a sense of respect and friendship. We have to "have each other's backs."

⭐ The Torah does not tell us what the pact between Jonathan and David consists of. What do you think it was? Jonathan gave David his sword, bow, and belt. What does it mean when you let someone use your baseball glove, phone, or something similar that is important to you? Have you ever given someone something that was very meaningful to you, simply to show that person how strongly you feel about them?

Teacher's tip: Letting someone use something important to you shows you trust them.

⭐ Do you notice the word *brit* here, which we translate as "pact"? In what other context does the word *brit* or *bris* come up? How are the two situations connected?

Teacher's tip: A *brit* or *bris* is the circumcision ceremony for Jewish boys. It means that we are born into a partnership with God. God's job is to create the world; our job is to do *mitzvot,* or sacred commandments, that help complete the world into a just and compassionate place. We are on the same team.

⭐ Do you think that a *brit* between two boys is different from a *brit* between a girl and a boy who are good friends?

Teacher's tip: Men are often willing to tell each other things that they may not tell women. It is not better or worse, just different.

In the Heat of the Moment

⭐ Have you ever seen anybody act crazy or get into a fight over a game? What do you think of the rioting that sometimes takes place after some professional sports games?

Teacher's tip: Riots have taken place after soccer matches and world championship games. Players also get carried away on the field. Part of the reason is because some aspects of competitive sports are forms of approved violence (think body checking in hockey). We feel an adrenaline rush and forget it is only a game.

⭐ Do you think it was right for the boy in this excerpt from *The Chosen* to tell the boy that he wanted to kill him, or should he have kept that thought to himself?

Teacher's tip: In this particular case in the novel, the two guys become close friends. By looking back and realizing how ridiculous they acted, it made room for an apology and forgiveness.

⭐ What would you have done if the guy who wanted to hit his friend on the head with his bat had told you what he had fantasized? Is this something that should be ignored? Reported? Discussed with someone else?

Teacher's tip: Every student will have a different reaction, but the bottom line is that if we feel there is the potential for violence, it must be reported.

⭐ Why do you think people get into fights over games?

Teacher's tip: People lose sight of what is important and get carried away by competition and adrenaline.

⭐ After a fight is over, do you walk away and ignore it? Do you talk to the person? How do you make things right again?

Teacher's tip: An essential part of competition is to "come back to reality," shake hands with an opponent, and be a gracious winner or loser. This transforms the game from being about winning to performing with excellence and drive.

Journaling Time: What Do I Think?

Give students quiet time to journal in the spaces provided in the book. If you are doing this with a group, remind them you will be reading these journals privately, and you will not share anything that is written with the group. Respect privacy.

Close the Lesson: Text Connection and Possible Activity

Choose one of the options explained under "Planning a Lesson."

True to Myself
Sometimes Things Bother Me, but I Am Not Comfortable Speaking Up

Goals

- To identify silence as a defense mechanism
- To name the "inner voice" of our conscience as our *yetzer hatov*
- To learn to listen to our *yetzer hatov* and speak up when necessary, such as when we feel something is wrong or when we need help

Hebrew Vocabulary

הָרִימִי בַּכֹּחַ קוֹלֵךְ...
הָרִימִי אַל־תִּירָאִי

Harimi vako'ach koleicha.... Harimi! Al tira'i!

Raise your voice with strength....
Lift it up! Do not be afraid!
—Isaiah 40:9

יֵצֶר הַטּוֹב
Yetzer hatov
Good impulse, conscience

יֵצֶר הָרָע
Yetzer hara
Bad impulse, animal instinct

Warm-up for Groups

Have each student create a paper airplane that best represents him. Provide color markers so that students can add designs. Have each guy present his airplane to the group.

Your Personal Story

Follow one of the three options explained under "Planning a Lesson."

Find Yourself a Friend

Ask students to read through the quotations from Jewish teenage guys in the book (pp. 39–41). Have them put a ✔ next to quotations they strongly agree with, an ✘ next to quotes they strongly disagree with, and ignore any in between. Have the guys share their ✔'s and ✘'s, and ask them why.

Select Something to Study: Did You Know?, Get Yourself a Teacher, and/or Learn

For "Did You Know?" and "Get Yourself a Teacher," see the relevant questions under "Planning a Lesson."

Learn

 ### Pick Someone Else!

⭐ What are some of the objections Moses has to God's choosing him?

Teacher's tip: He feels inadequate ("who am I ... ?"), he doesn't think anyone will listen to him, and he doesn't feel he is good with words.

⭐ Why is it hard to speak up? What is Moses (or anyone else) afraid of?

Teacher's tip: Speaking up makes us vulnerable. It risks revealing how we really feel, and we are afraid people will laugh at us or reject us.

✡ What could God have said to give Moses more confidence?

Teacher's tip: God said that God will be with Moses and gives him proof to help him on his mission. Also, though not in the text cited, God sends Moses's brother, Aaron, to help him. Bringing a friend or sibling can give us courage.

✡ When do you feel confident? When don't you? What can you do to be more confident?

Teacher's tip: We are usually more confident doing something we are used to with people we know. We lose confidence doing something new or when we feel alone. We often hide behind silence, but silence is often a form of consent.

 ## Finding Good, Finding Confidence

✡ When do you feel down or depressed?

Teacher's tip: This is personal to each student. Feeling depressed occasionally is normal. (Note: Depression can be serious. If you suspect anything more significant than the average "the blues" you should contact the student's parents/guardians and recommend seeking professional and/or medical help.)

✡ What do you do to make yourself feel better when you are feeling down?

Teacher's tip: Physical activity, music, and hanging out with friends are usual ways to combat depression. Also, doing something good for someone else can help lift our spirits.

✡ Over the past week, what is something good that you did for someone else? Focus on that good thing. That is who you really are!

Teacher's tip: Push students to find at least one thing, even if you have to go through the schedule day by day.

✡ Music can help us find our voice. Rabbi Nachman teaches that each of us has our own song that comes from our higher selves. What song or piece of music means a lot to you? Why?

Teacher's tip: Be willing to listen to contemporary music you do not know, and ask to read the lyrics.

Journaling Time: What Do I Think?

Give students quiet time to journal in the spaces provided in the book. If you are doing this with a group, remind them you will be reading these journals privately, and you will not share anything that is written with the group. Respect privacy.

Close the Lesson: Text Connection and Possible Activity

Choose one of the options explained under "Planning a Lesson."

One Day Son, This Will All Be Yours

I Love My Parents, but Adults Can Be Clueless

Goals

- ✡ To validate feelings of frustration with parents
- ✡ To identify fear as a usual motivation for parents' actions
- ✡ To explain the concept of *bitachon* as trust and discuss earning trust
- ✡ To provide positive role models of parents and sons honoring each other

Hebrew Vocabulary

בִּטָּחוֹן
Bitachon
Trust

אַהֲבָה
Ahavah
Love

Warm-up for Groups

Have students play a memory game: When I move out of my parent(s)' house, the one thing I will be sure to take with me is my…. Have each student explain what it is and why it is important to him. When everyone is done explaining their items, each student then has to go back and name what all of the previous people shared, in order. You as facilitator may want to go last as it will be the longest list and it will show that you care about each of them.

Your Personal Story

Follow one of the three options explained under "Planning a Lesson."

Find Yourself a Friend

Ask students to read through the quotations from Jewish teenage guys in the book (pp. 54–57). Have them put a ✔ next to quotations they strongly agree with, an ✘ next to quotes they strongly disagree with, and ignore any in between. Have the guys share their ✔'s and ✘'s, and ask them why.

Select Something to Study: Did You Know?, Get Yourself a Teacher, and/or Learn

For "Did You Know?" and "Get Yourself a Teacher," see the relevant questions under "Planning a Lesson."

Learn

 ### Here I Am

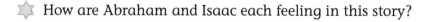

☆ How are Abraham and Isaac each feeling in this story?

Teacher's tip: Each one is trapped in his own story. They are probably feeling very anxious and have fear of the unknown.

☆ Why doesn't Abraham tell Isaac more about what is happening?

Teacher's tip: Abraham could possibly be in shock. He could also be feeling faith that God will ultimately do what is best.

☆ Why does the story repeat the phrases "my father" and "my son"? What does this do to the drama of the story?

Teacher's tip: These phrases highlight the closeness of their relationship. It heightens the drama of the story and raises tension.

⭐ The dialogue and journey begins with a description of Abraham and Isaac going off together and ends with the phrase "both of them went together." What is ironic about this phrase?

Teacher's tip: While they are physically side by side, they are mentally in different worlds. Abraham is thinking about what God has asked him to do. Isaac is thinking of getting an animal for sacrifice.

⭐ When do you have the most meaningful conversations with your parent(s)? What questions would you like to ask them?

Teacher's tip: Many conversations happen with parents in the car. This way we do not have to make eye contact with each other. Sometimes a conversation can happen while playing a sport or over a meal. Many boys are afraid to ask their parents some personal questions.

⭐ Today, people risk their lives when they enlist in the military. Can you think of other times you would risk yourself for something you believe in?

Teacher's tip: People regularly risk their lives in the military or in rescue professions. We risk our lives for things we believe in more often than we might think.

In My Father's Shadow

⭐ Do you sometimes feel that you are being "sacrificed" to your parent(s)' plans or hopes?

Teacher's tip: Personal answers will follow, but often parents have hopes and expectations, and things rarely turn out as planned.

⭐ What do you think is the effect the near-sacrifice of Isaac has on his future relationship with his father?

Teacher's tip: We do not see any written interaction between Abraham and Isaac after this event in the Torah. Abraham returns to Beer Sheva, but it does not say Isaac goes with him. Isaac does appear at the funeral of his father. It is possible that Isaac was angry and chose to separate from his father, making this part of the story a tragedy.

✡ Psychologist Sam Osherson claims that many men suffer from "father hunger," which is the need to know who our fathers really are (or were, if deceased) and how they felt during their childhoods. Does this make sense to you? Why or why not?

Teacher's tip: Sons naturally want to know what their fathers "really think" and seek their approval. If a father is the so-called strong, silent type, then a son can be left guessing.

✡ Some men have been raised to believe that they should be unemotional with their children, particularly their sons. In most cases, children with fathers such as these develop their own difficulties in communicating. Can you imagine why?

Teacher's tip: Many men of an older generation were taught to be independent, competitive, stoic, and strong. Silence was a way of proving you were stronger than your emotions. Men today are often in a different culture of expressiveness, cooperation, and greater interpersonal skills. There is often a potential gap of communication between fathers and sons.

Roles and Role Models

✡ The Talmud notices a change in the word order of the Torah when it comes to mothers and fathers. The first parent is named to make up for a natural imbalance. Do you think it is true that mothers are the ones sons can talk to more easily? Do you think it is true that sons naturally revere or fear their fathers? Why or why not?

Teacher's tip: Western culture makes it permissible for mothers to communicate more freely with children and for fathers to be disciplinarians. This stereotype is changing, expanding the culturally acceptable ways for men to express themselves.

✡ The Rabbis understand "revere" as respecting and not embarrassing a father. Do you think this holds true today? When might a parent feel embarrassed? When does your parent embarrass you?

Teacher's tip: Fathers get embarrassed just like anyone else, but they often try not to show it. Similarly, children get embarrassed as they try to break away from their parents and establish themselves independently.

✡ Have you ever been told not to sit in a particular seat because it "belongs" to the father or grandfather? When did that happen?

Teacher's tip: Many people today have their own formal chair at meals, especially holiday meals. Fathers are often expected to sit at the head of the table.

✡ How do you express your love for your parents?

Teacher's tip: Identify both verbal and non-verbal ways of showing love.

✡ The Rabbis interpret "honor" for when your parents are older and you might have to take care of them. Can you imagine being in that position? How might you handle it?

Teacher's tip: This will be very difficult for adolescents to imagine, but they may be seeing parents role-modeling this situation now with grandparents.

✡ Many people say that children repeat what their own parents did when they were children. Do you think this will be true of you? In what ways? In what ways not?

Teacher's tip: Invite students to think of things they would like to emulate from their parents and things they would like to leave behind. Let them know that to a certain extent they have the power to make choices.

 ## Paternal Job Description

✡ What do you think of the Talmud's list of obligations of a father to a son? What is surprising? What, in your opinion, is missing?

Teacher's tip: A usual source of surprise is that "love" is missing. This is most likely because it is either taken for granted or because legally it cannot be measured, but providing an education and skills can. The Talmud seems to be focusing on the physical here, not the emotional. However, many of these actions can be read symbolically with great emotional meaning.

✡ Circumcise: This means not only *brit milah*, but also sometimes a parent causes his/her child necessary pain. What pain do you think you have to suffer in order to grow?

Teacher's tip: Everyone experiences pain and loss as part of growing up. Think of things you had to do that scared you: being dropped off somewhere for the first time, riding a bicycle, learning to swim, or learning something difficult.

✡ Redeem: Traditionally, first-born sons were supposed to serve in the Temple in Jerusalem. A father "redeemed" his baby boy when he reached thirty days of age by paying for him to be released from this obligation. Some people think that *pidyon ha-ben*, the name of this ceremony, keeps the child from being overwhelmed with a task he cannot handle. When is a time your parent(s) kept you from doing something because you weren't ready?

Teacher's tip: The parents' job is to protect their children from unnecessary pain and standing up for them. This may mean defending them against an unfair situation with a teacher or coach, keeping them from doing something they want to do too early, or giving them aid when they are overwhelmed.

✡ Teach him Torah: In the Rabbis' time, this referred to all education. Is school something that is a source of agreement or conflict between you and your parent(s)? What about Hebrew school? The obligation to educate your son may be translated into the obligation to pay for college education or even for a graduate education like law or medical school. When do you think the father's obligation ends?

Teacher's tip: Some students love school and achieve easily, and some are not natural students. Hebrew school that takes place after school or on weekends often means students are also tired, hungry, and under pressure to do homework. This creates pressure and often translates into conflict between parents' expectations and students' desires.

Future expectations also will vary from student to student, from students who do not go to college to those who are expected to work their way through college, to students who must go to a local or state school because of money to students who are fortunate enough to apply to many schools. This is also an opportunity to bring up the possibility of a gap year spent in Israel.

✡ Take a wife for him: We are long past the age of arranged marriages. But would you ever go to your parent(s) for advice on relationships?

Teacher's tip: Parents are usually the last people a son would go to for relationship advice, but parents can often surprise you.

Teach him a craft and teach him to swim: Contemporary parents eventually want you to be self-sufficient. What are some areas where you are more independent than you were a few years ago? In what areas do you imagine you will be more independent next year? When do you want a parent's help? When don't you?

Teacher's tip: Answers will vary from student to student. This question will bring up the idea that guys usually both want and do not want a parent's help, which can confuse a parent fairly easily.

Journaling Time: What Do I Think?

Give students quiet time to journal in the spaces provided in the book. If you are doing this with a group, remind them you will be reading these journals privately, and you will not share anything that is written with the group. Respect privacy.

Close the Lesson: Text Connection and Possible Activity

Choose one of the options explained under "Planning a Lesson."

God ... Really?

I'm Not Sure I Believe in God Because the World Is Pretty Messed Up

Goals

- To realize it is okay to redefine the word "God" to mean something personally meaningful
- To survey the many different ways Judaism has defined God
- To acknowledge that faith is often a struggle

Hebrew Vocabulary

שְׁמַע יִשְׂרָאֵל יְיָ אֱלֹהֵינוּ יְיָ אֶחָד

Sh'ma Yisrael: Adonai Eloheinu Adonai echad.

Listen, member of the people Israel: the Eternal is our God, the Eternal is one.
—**Deuteronomy 6:4**

הֲלָכָה
Halacha
Jewish law

Warm-up for Groups

Show the eight-minute video *Cosmic Zoom*, a short film directed by Eva Szasz and produced by the National Film Board of Canada in 1968. While the animation is dated, it will set the stage for talking about God. Ask students:

> According to the video, what is at the end of outer space?
>
> What is at the end of inner space?

Teacher's tip: The answer to both questions is: Nothing. One of the names for God in Hebrew is *Ayin*, or Nothingness. Another name is *Ein Sof*, or Infinity.

Your Personal Story

Follow one of the three options explained under "Planning a Lesson."

Find Yourself a Friend

Ask students to read through the quotations from Jewish teenage guys in the book (pp. 75–78). Have them put a ✔ next to quotations they strongly agree with, an ✘ next to quotes they strongly disagree with, and ignore any in between. Have the guys share their ✔'s and ✘'s, and ask them why.

Select Something to Study: Did You Know?, Get Yourself a Teacher, and/or Learn

For "Did You Know?" and "Get Yourself a Teacher," see the relevant questions under "Planning a Lesson."

Learn

 My God and God of My Ancestors

 Why do you think it is important that each person has his own understanding of God?

Teacher's tip: Each person is unique and has his own truth of his experience.

Why is it important to understand the faith of your ancestors?

Teacher's tip: People who came before us often had the same hopes and fears, and together there is a great deal of combined wisdom.

How did you understand God when you were a child? How do you understand God in synagogue today? Out in the street in your regular life? How might you think of God in the future?

Teacher's tip: By illustrating the idea that how we understand God can change depending upon time and place, we can be flexible with how we define God for ourselves in the future. There are no wrong answers here.

Author of the World

What do you think of Bachya ibn Pakuda's demonstration of God? Is it convincing?

Teacher's tip: Whether or not people find it convincing is personal, but this is a common kind of argument known as an argument from design. An argument from design is when someone argues that because there is order in the universe, it implies that there is Someone who made it that way. The same way a watch implies a watchmaker, according to this argument, the laws of nature in the world imply a Creator.

Can you find any flaws in his argument?

Teacher's tip: Bachya's words are a demonstration, not proof. It will only be convincing if someone chooses to believe that the universe is not completely random.

When you look at nature, do you think there is a design or purpose?

Teacher's tip: Again, this is personal but, according to Judaism, creation has a purpose, which is to acknowledge and appreciate God and the world.

 ## Traditional Beliefs

 Do you think that people who don't believe all of these ideas should stop calling themselves Jewish? Why or why not?

Teacher's tip: You can be Jewish and not have traditional beliefs. In fact, many liberal denominations of Judaism reject certain traditional beliefs, such as the resurrection of the dead or that the Oral Torah, the teachings of the Rabbis, are God given.

 If you were to make a list of the most important ingredients of Judaism, what would they be?

Teacher's tip: Students should try to speak from their experience. If, however, they want to only cite the Golden Rule—"treat others the way you want to be treated" — challenge them as to what is Jewish about that. You may want to look to chapter 10 in *The JGuy's Guide* for a more comprehensive list of commandments that include not only ethics but also holidays, life-cycle events, and everyday holiness.

Journaling Time: What Do I Think?

Give students quiet time to journal in the spaces provided in the book. If you are doing this with a group, remind them you will be reading these journals privately, and you will not share anything that is written with the group. Respect privacy.

Close the Lesson: Text Connection and Possible Activity

Choose one of the options explained under "Planning a Lesson."

The Torah of Everything
Now that I Think about It, That's Amazing!

Goals

- ✡ To see Jewish spirituality in everyday living
- ✡ To bring a Jewish perspective to activities guys are already doing, such as sports and games
- ✡ To introduce wonder as an essential Jewish concept and attitude toward life

Hebrew Vocabulary

מָה־רַבּוּ מַעֲשֶׂיךָ יְיָ כֻּלָּם בְּחָכְמָה
עָשִׂיתָ מָלְאָה הָאָרֶץ קִנְיָנֶךָ

*Mah rabu ma'asecha Adonai!
Kulam b'chochmah asita; mal'ah
ha'aretz kinyanecha.*

Adonai, You have made so much! In
wisdom You have made them all; the
Earth is full of Your creations.
—Psalm 104:24

בָּרוּךְ אַתָּה יְיָ אֱלֹהֵינוּ מֶלֶךְ הָעוֹלָם
שֶׁהֶחֱיָנוּ וְקִיְּמָנוּ וְהִגִּיעָנוּ לַזְּמַן הַזֶּה

**Baruch atah Adonai eloheinu melech haolam
shehechianu v'kiy'manu v'higiyanu lazman hazeh.**

Blessed are You, Adonai our god, Ruler of the Universe,
who gives us life, sustains us,
and enables us to reach this moment.

צַדִּיק	בְּרָכָה	תִּקּוּן עוֹלָם
Tzadik	*Bracha*	*Tikkun olam*
A righteous teacher	Blessing	Repair of the world

Warm-up for Groups

Have students divide into teams. Have them play a game of checkers, Team A against
Team B, with a representative from each team taking turns to make the next move.
This will become relevant under one of the "Learn" texts below.

Your Personal Story

Follow one of the three options explained under "Planning a Lesson."

Find Yourself a Friend

Ask students to read through the quotations from Jewish teenage guys in the book
(pp. 91–93). Have them put a ✔ next to quotations they strongly agree with, an ✘
next to quotes they strongly disagree with, and ignore any in between. Have the guys
share their ✔'s and ✘'s, and ask them why.

For "Did You Know?" and "Get Yourself a Teacher," see the relevant questions under "Planning a Lesson."

Learn

The Rules of Checkers

⭐ What do you think of the first two rules—that you can only make one move at a time and you can't go backward? What does this teach you? Do you agree with these ideas?

Teacher's tip: In an age when we want to do everything all the time, the rule of one move at a time reminds us we have to choose, and every choice means not choosing something else. Our lives are ultimately the sum of the choices we make.

⭐ Describe a time when it would have been helpful to remember these rules in your life.

Teacher's tip: Encourage students to think of times when they have made choices where there was no going back.

⭐ What do you think the last rule—when you get to the end you can move anywhere you want—means?

Teacher's tip: This can mean many things, such as in old age you just don't care as much about consequences as you once did, or that in the World-to-Come (if you believe in it) you can do whatever you want.

Rules for Living Wisely

⭐ Do you agree with *Kohelet's* approach to life? Why or why not?

Teacher's tip: Kohelet's approach to life is realistic and helpful for getting satisfaction out of each day. It is very practical: eat and drink well, do what you enjoy, and don't be alone.

✡ Judaism believes in doing more than just surviving. Is *Kohelet's* recipe for living satisfactory? How does *tikkun olam*—repairing and transforming the world—fit in?

Teacher's tip: Kohelet's teaching is about savoring life and surviving difficulties; it does not talk about fixing the world or changing society for the better. An important part of Judaism is the belief that we can also improve our lives and our communities. In this way, from a Jewish point of view, *Kohelet* is realistic but incomplete.

✡ What do you think *Kohelet* means by stating, "Your action was long ago approved by God"?

Teacher's tip: According to *Kohelet*, God wants us to have fun, enjoy life, and not be alone!

 ## Omnipresent God

✡ This teaching tells us that everything, even a stone, is part of God. We don't worship stones, but we can see them as pieces of something bigger. Here, Moses Cordovero's words are reminding us that when we use words like "King" to refer to God, God is not really a king but an indescribable infinity that fills and surrounds the universe. You can see God in nature or everyday objects. Does this kind of understanding of God speak to you? Why or why not?

Teacher's tip: When we talk about God, we are using symbolic language. It is ultimately impossible to limit God to words. Instead, we talk of things that represent ideas of God.

✡ Replace the word "stone" in this teaching with some object in your home, such as a computer, glass of water, soccer ball, or musical instrument. Does this change how you look at the world?

Teacher's tip: Anything can be amazing if you don't take it for granted and look at it the right way. We can choose to see the world through eyes of wonder.

✡ Choose an ordinary object in the room. Explain why it is amazing when you stop and think about it.

Teacher's tip: This is a practical exercise that can be very helpful. It can remind us to see the world through an attitude of wonder.

✡ Why should we pay attention to these everyday actions?

Teacher's tip: Everyday actions are often ones we take for granted, but people with disabilities cannot. When we pay attention to everyday activities and the amazing things our bodies and minds are capable of doing we can cultivate feelings of gratitude.

✡ What might blessings remind us of as we go through our daily routine?

Teacher's tip: Developing mindfulness gives us feelings of thankfulness, amazement, and appreciation. It helps us pay attention and live life more deeply.

✡ What kind of life would we live if we tried to live by Rabbi Meir's rule of aspiring to say one hundred blessings a day?

Teacher's tip: This would be a life of great mindfulness, where we try to pay attention and not take things for granted.

✡ Do you think trying to say a hundred blessings each day will interfere with other things you want to do, or will it make life more meaningful?

Teacher's tip: If we try to say blessings for the purpose of checking off a list or fulfilling an obligation, then saying a hundred blessings a day can be a burden. If it is a natural way of experiencing the world with wonder, it can enhance joy.

✡ Some believe a blessing only counts if someone says "Amen" after you say it. How does this complicate things? Why do you think some believe this is a requirement?

Teacher's tip: On one hand, having someone say "Amen" means you share the experience. On the other hand, you can also experience wonder alone.

✡ If you were to write your own blessing for something that happens to you each day, what would it be?

Teacher's tip: According to Jewish law, we are not supposed to write our own blessings. Liberal denominations of Judaism have ignored this rule, saying it helps us apply an attitude of wonder to daily living.

Journaling Time: What Do I Think?

Give students quiet time to journal in the spaces provided in the book. If you are doing this with a group, remind them you will be reading these journals privately, and you will not share anything that is written with the group. Respect privacy.

Close the Lesson: Text Connection and Possible Activity

Choose one of the options explained under "Planning a Lesson."

Enough Already
Why Am I So Stressed Out?

Goals

- ⭐ To identify our culture as one of workaholism and radical multi-tasking
- ⭐ To explore Shabbat as a healthy response to stress
- ⭐ To redefine Shabbat not as a day but as a break to renew oneself

Hebrew Vocabulary

וַיְכַל אֱלֹהִים בַּיּוֹם
הַשְּׁבִיעִי מְלַאכְתּוֹ אֲשֶׁר עָשָׂה

*Vay'chal Elohim bayom hash'vi'i
m'lachto asher asah.*

God ceased work on the seventh day.
—Genesis 2:2

שַׁבָּת
Shabbat
The Sabbath

Warm-up for Groups

As an introduction to this lesson, which is about being busy and able to slow down to look someone in the eye, have students walk around the room as fast as they can without hitting each other or running into anything. Tell them they are in the middle of a city and have a very important place to be. After a minute, tell them to start to slow down and notice the faces of the people around them but keep walking. After another minute, have them stop in front of a person, look him in the eye, and give him a high-five or fist-bump. Then have everyone take a seat.

Your Personal Story

Follow one of the three options explained under "Planning a Lesson."

Find Yourself a Friend

Ask students to read through the quotations from Jewish teenage guys in the book (pp. 109–111). Have them put a ✔ next to quotations they strongly agree with, an ✗ next to quotes they strongly disagree with, and ignore any in between. Have the guys share their ✔'s and ✗'s, and ask them why.

Select Something to Study: Did You Know?, Get Yourself a Teacher, and/or Learn

For "Did You Know?" and "Get Yourself a Teacher," see the relevant questions under "Planning a Lesson."

Working to Live or Living to Work?

⭐ Do you find yourself thinking of work, chores, and homework during times when you should be relaxing, being with friends, or on vacation? When did this start? Does it bother you?

Teacher's tip: This is an opportunity for students to tell a personal story about a growing homework load or the pressure to get into college. It could also be an opportunity to talk about whether sports or some other activity allow them to "let off steam" or are simply more stressful to fit into their schedules.

⭐ When are you most stressed out?

Teacher's tip: In addition to the obvious answers—when faced with lots of homework or before a test at school—you can ask them if there are any people in their lives that stress them out and why. What do you think a good balance between living and working would look like?

Teacher's tip: Emphasize the need for hang-out time.

⭐ According to this teaching, Shabbat is not just about one day out of seven but about energy in each day. When during the day can you stop and take a "Shabbat-moment"?

Teacher's tip: Suggest taking a moment to take a walk or listen to music.

 ## Disconnect in Order to Connect

⭐ Do you think it is realistic to "set apart one day a week for freedom"? Why or why not?

Teacher's tip: Many people think this is unrealistic, but reassure students it is possible.

⭐ What do you think Rabbi Heschel means when he says we try to dominate the world, but during Shabbat we try to dominate the self?

Teacher's tip: Dominating the world means being "successful" at things like grades, sports, performances, and jobs. These things bring us recognition, ego gratification, and money. Dominating the self is about making sure we live the life we want to be leading. If we do so, we feel content and that life is meaningful. It is easy to confuse the two.

✡ What are some to the best things about computers and mobile phones? What are some of the drawbacks? How do they make life easier? How do they increase stress? Why do you think Rabbi Heschel calls these things "which have been so easily turned into weapons of destruction"? What is being destroyed?

Teacher's tip: Computers and mobile phones give us practically unlimited access to each other and the world. However, people have confused "sharing" with "connecting." Being available 24/7 can be stressful. And communicating can be wonderful ("I love you") or it can be destructive ("I hate you"). One of the problems with email, text messages, electronic social networking, and mobile devices is that we can communicate instantly, but sometimes we send something before we have thought it through.

✡ If you could have an hour each day without chores, errands, or homework and could do anything, what would you do? Who would you do it with?

Teacher's tip: An hour that is chore, errand, and homework free can be liberating and transformative. Everyone deserves a Shabbat hour each day.

 ## Hey Moses! Stop, Look, and Listen!

✡ The Torah says, "When Adonai saw that he had turned aside to look ..." Focusing on these words, what was the test God had devised for Moses?

Teacher's tip: God's test was to see if Moses could pay attention and notice something that was easy to walk by or dismiss.

✡ How long do you think it would have taken Moses to notice that the bush was not burning up? Would he have immediately understood what was happening or would it have taken some time to observe?

Teacher's tip: It would take a while to notice that something is burning but not burning up. Moses must have sat and watched it for a few minutes at least. Paying attention takes time.

✡ If Moses had been listening to music, texting, and riding by in his SUV, do you think Moses would have noticed the burning bush? Why or why not? What might this say about us and our lives today?

Teacher's tip: Moses would have missed the miracle if he had been multi-tasking. We are probably missing miracles, too.

✡ In this episode, the Torah teaches that learning to stop and pay attention is a primary spiritual step. Do you agree? Why or why not?

Teacher's tip: This is a personal opinion, but if we cannot stop and give another person, nature, or ourselves our undivided attention, we will miss experiencing feelings of wonder.

✡ Can you think of an instance when you had time to stop and notice something that you might otherwise have missed?

Teacher's tip: If necessary, send students outside to look for "fingerprints" of God. Dissect a flower. Look at stars. Observe an insect. Feel amazement.

Journaling Time: What Do I Think?

Give students quiet time to journal in the spaces provided in the book. If you are doing this with a group, remind them you will be reading these journals privately, and you will not share anything that is written with the group. Respect privacy.

Close the Lesson: Text Connection and Possible Activity

Choose one of the options explained under "Planning a Lesson."

Falling in Lust, Falling in Love

I Can't Help Thinking about Sex, but I Don't Know What's Right for Me

Author's note: For this lesson, you may want to alert parents ahead of time about the topic. If they are uncomfortable, they can keep their child at home for this discussion.

Goals

- To identify myths around teenage guys and sexuality
- To see sex within limits as a potentially healthy activity approved by Judaism
- To name unhealthy sexual activities
- To identify Jewish values that are part of a sex ethic
- To promote inclusion of gay, lesbian, transgender, bisexual, and questioning people

Hebrew Vocabulary

קְדֹשִׁים תִּהְיוּ

K'doshim tih'yu.

You shall be holy.
—**Leviticus 19:2**

אֱמֶת	צְנִיעוּת	קְדוּשָׁה
Emet	*Tz'niyut*	*K'dushah*
Honesty	Modesty and privacy	Holiness, to be exclusively set apart for a higher purpose

בְּרִיאוּת	בְּרִית	
B'riyut	*B'rit*	
Health	Covenantal relationship	

מִשְׁפָּט	שִׂמְחָה	כְּתוּבָּה
Mishpat	*Simchah*	*Ketubah*
Fairness	Joy	Marriage agreement

מִשְׁפָּחָה	אַהֲבָה
Mishpachah	*Ahavah*
Family	Love (including self-esteem, caring, support, and empathy)

Warm-up for Groups

Invite students, all at the same time, to write down every slang word for "sex" that they know on a large piece of paper or poster board. Nothing is forbidden. In this lesson, we are going to talk about Jewish views on lust, love, and being a man. (Make sure to dispose of the poster when you are done.)

Your Personal Story

Follow one of the three options explained under "Planning a Lesson."

Find Yourself a Friend

Ask students to read through the quotations from Jewish teenage guys in the book (pp. 127–128). Have them put a ✔ next to quotations they strongly agree with, an ✗ next to quotes they strongly disagree with, and ignore any in between. Have the guys share their ✔'s and ✗'s, and ask them why.

For "Did You Know?" and "Get Yourself a Teacher," see the relevant questions under "Planning a Lesson."

Learn

 What Is the Story of the Snake and the Fruit Really About?

✡ In this story, sex and knowledge are closely linked. In the Hebrew Bible, Adam "knowing" Eve is a euphemism for sex. Sex is intended to be an act of intimacy, to "know in the biblical sense." Why does intimacy make sex special? What do you think happens if there is sex without intimacy, without really knowing someone?

Teacher's tip: Distinguish between sex as an act of lust versus sex as an act of intimacy. The former does not involve a relationship; the latter does. Judaism understands sex in terms of a sacred relationship.

✡ This story is also about "firsts." You only get one first. What changes in Adam and Eve after this first sexual act? What might that mean for us?

Teacher's tip: Adam and Eve are forever changed after their first sexual encounter, and so are we. They become self-conscious and more aware of their bodies. They also share an important experience.

✡ God tells Adam not to rush ahead and eat the fruit, but the snake says to go for it. What are the pressures today to have sex sooner rather than later? What are some good reasons to wait?

Teacher's tip: Urges to have sex include everything from feelings of lust and curiosity to genuine love. Delaying helps clarify what is a healthy activity in relation to Jewish values.

 Where Did Adam and Eve Have Sex?

✡ Why do you think Rashi made his comment about where Cain was conceived? How else might the story be understood?

Teacher's tip: Rashi was reacting to a specific Christian environment that saw sex as sinful and chastity as virtuous. He is engaging in an argument that Adam and Eve's sex act was done in purity, and therefore there is nothing inherently sinful about sex. Of course, the story could be read that they had sex and got kicked out of the Garden as well.

> ✡ Does Rashi's comment change what you originally thought about the story? If yes, how so?

Teacher's tip: The usual interpretation is that Adam and Eve's sin exiled them from the Garden. Another way of looking at it is that a necessary consequence of sex is that we leave a part of childhood behind. The story is about a necessary loss of innocence through sex, not sin.

> ✡ Why do you think sex is often linked with the ideas of sin, guilt, and embarrassment?

Teacher's tip: Having sex too soon or with the wrong person usually brings with it feelings of wrong-doing, guilt, and embarrassment. The key is to delay and to act only on core values.

Rape and Seeing Woman as More than Body Parts

> ✡ What do you think of the revenge that Simon and Levi undertook against the people of Shechem? Should they have killed the rapist? Should they have killed all the townsmen? Why do you think they did so? Should a lot of people be punished for one person's misdeeds?

Teacher's tip: The rage of Simon and Levi is understandable because their sister was raped. However, we have laws precisely to make sure we don't make mistakes and people get just punishments. There are also degrees of responsibility, and the consequences should fit the crime.

> ✡ What do you think Dinah was feeling and thinking? What would you have wanted to happen if you were her?

Teacher's tip: It is critical to point out that Dinah is silent. We need to listen to women's voices. Contemporary author Anita Diamant wrote the best-selling novel *The Red Tent* from the point of view of Dinah.

✡ What would you say to someone who claimed that Dinah brought the rape upon herself (as rape victims are so often accused of doing)? Does any woman or girl cause her own rape?

Teacher's tip: Rape is never the victim's fault. A woman or girl never causes her own rape. Dressing or acting in a sexually provocative manner is not an invitation to rape.

✡ What do you think is the appropriate punishment for rape?

Teacher's tip: Our society sends people to jail for rape. We do not believe in castration or the death penalty for the crime. Some cultures have historically punished rape this way, and this story is evidence of it being part of our ancient history. Today in the United States the death penalty is used almost exclusively as punishment for murder, and mutilation of any kind is illegal.

✡ Have you learned about date rape, sometimes called acquaintance rape or drug-facilitated sexual assault?

Teacher's tip: Being drunk or high is not an excuse to touch another person sexually. Even if someone is acting in a provocative way, sexual activity must always be consensual. Sexual assault and rape are terrible crimes with long-lasting effects. Encourage guys to always be sober and aware, be clear in their relationships, and stay with groups of people they know and trust. Once we have condemned rape as wrong, guys must be aware of their own behavior. Rape is an act of violence and aggression. It is completely antithetical to a Jewish understanding of sex. In addition, if someone is under the influence of alcohol or drugs, their "consent" does not count. It is not okay to have sex with someone who is out-of-their-mind drunk, for example, no matter what she or he says.

Journaling Time: What Do I Think?

Give students quiet time to journal in the spaces provided in the book. If you are doing this with a group, remind them you will be reading these journals privately, and you will not share anything that is written with the group. Respect privacy.

Close the Lesson: Text Connection and Possible Activity

Choose one of the options explained under "Planning a Lesson."

Not on My Watch
Does What I Do Actually Matter?

Goals

- ⭐ To empower students that they can make a difference
- ⭐ To identify Jewish values around social justice
- ⭐ To name Jewish organizations with which they might want to get involved and role models they can emulate

Hebrew Vocabulary

לֹא תַעֲמֹד עַל־דַּם רֵעֶךָ

Lo ta'amod al dam rei'echa.

You may not stand by while your neighbor bleeds.
—Leviticus 19:16

צְדָקָה
Tzedakah
Righteous giving

Warm-up for Groups

Put a paper plate on the floor. Give the physical challenge that everyone has to have one part of his body on the plate at the same time. Once students have done it, tell them that the paper plate is the world, and with more and more people, we have to find a way to share our resources. This lesson is about creating a just world.

Your Personal Story

Follow one of the three options explained under "Planning a Lesson."

Find Yourself a Friend

Ask students to read through the quotations from Jewish teenage guys in the book (pp. 148–149). Have them put a ✔ next to quotations they strongly agree with, an ✘ next to quotes they strongly disagree with, and ignore any in between. Have the guys share their ✔'s and ✘'s, and ask them why.

Select Something to Study: Did You Know?, Get Yourself a Teacher, and/or Learn

For "Did You Know?" and "Get Yourself a Teacher," see the relevant questions under "Planning a Lesson."

Learn

 ### The Prophets: The First Social Justice Activists

✡ Identify some of the problems the prophets were criticizing in society. What did they say was offensive to God?

Teacher' tip: Pretending to be religious while also being unjust or tolerating injustice is offensive to God. The prophets were not only criticizing unfair treatment of the vulnerable but the hypocrisy of so-called religious people.

✡ Which of these quotations speaks to you the most? Why?

Teacher's tip: Give students time to reread the quotations.

⬥ If you were to identify a modern-day prophet, who would it be? Why? Is there anyone living today who you think qualifies?

Teacher's tip: Common answers are Martin Luther King Jr., Gandhi, and Nelson Mandela. Push them to think of other, less grandiose figures, or even their peers.

 ## Moses Maimonides' Rules on How to Give to a Poor Person

⬥ Moses Maimonides wanted people to act a certain way if they saw a beggar on the street. What are his main rules for conduct?

Teacher's tip: Maimonides is concerned with following through on the need to give, doing so in a virtuous and unselfish manner, and protecting the dignity of the recipient.

⬥ Why do you think he wrote that if you give something with "a scowl," you have lost any merit in giving?

Teacher's tip: Causing someone to despair can make him or her give up on life. Humiliation is a form of violence.

⬥ Why do you think Maimonides says that if you don't have anything to give, you should still say something comforting? Do you think you would be comfortable doing so?

Teacher's tip: Many homeless people simply want to be acknowledged and treated as human beings, not as objects or animals. Making a brief connection with a kind word can help restore their sense of humanity.

⬥ If you see a beggar on the street, would you give him or her a dollar? Why or why not? What are some alternatives to giving on the street?

Teacher's tip: If we are unwilling to give on the street, then we should make sure that we give institutionally or volunteer for an organization that combats hunger and poverty. We are not allowed to opt out of *tzedakah* altogether just because one form of it makes us uncomfortable.

A Prayer by Rabbi Jack Riemer

✡ Where is God when so many people are messing up the world? This prayer tries to answer that question. What is this prayer's answer?

Teacher's tip: This prayer puts the responsibility for making the world a better place back on people. When people ask, "Where is God?" this prayer answers, "Where are you?"

✡ This prayer imagines a partnership between people and God. What is God's part in making the world? What is our part?

Teacher's tip: According to this prayer, God's job is to create the world, and our job is to finish it by making it a place of justice and compassion.

✡ Have you ever thought of the connection between praying and doing? Is it enough just to pray?

Teacher's tip: In Judaism, it is never enough just to pray. Prayer is a prelude to action. We say a blessing, and then we do something immediately afterwards, whether it is eating a piece of bread or helping another person.

Journaling Time: What Do I Think?

Give students quiet time to journal in the spaces provided in the book. If you are doing this with a group, remind them you will be reading these journals privately, and you will not share anything that is written with the group. Respect privacy.

Close the Lesson: Text Connection and Possible Activity

Choose one of the options explained under "Planning a Lesson."

Looking Inside at the Man I Want to Be

Beginning with Myself

Goals

- ✡ To understand being a Jewish man as being a *mensch*

- ✡ To identify *mitzvot* (divine commandments) and *derech eretz* (civility)

- ✡ To explore ways *mitzvot* connect us to something greater than ourselves

- ✡ To learn Jewish texts focusing on introspection and character development

Hebrew Vocabulary

מִצְוָה גּוֹרֶרֶת מִצְוָה, וַעֲבֵרָה גּוֹרֶרֶת עֲבֵרָה

**Mitzvah goreret mitzvah,
va'aveirah goreret aveirah.**

One mitzvah will bring another mitzvah,
one sin will bring another sin.
—*Pirkei Avot 4:2*

מִצְוָה	טַלִּית	דֶּרֶךְ אֶרֶץ
Mitzvah	*Tallit*	*Derech eretz*
Divine commandment	Prayer shawl	Being civil

Warm-up for Groups

Show videos or photos of stereotypes of "tough guy" men in the media, then do a card pass: Give students two index cards, each of a different color. On one color, have each student write three characteristics of what he thinks the media, advertising, movies, and television shows say a "real man" is. On the other color, have him write three characteristics of what *he* thinks a "real man" is. Take back the cards and shuffle them. Redistribute them, and have students read them aloud, first the ones about the media, and then the ones with their personal opinions.

Your Personal Story

Follow one of the three options explained under "Planning a Lesson."

Find Yourself a Friend

Ask students to read through the quotations from Jewish teenage guys in the book (pp. 165–166). Have them put a ✔ next to quotations they strongly agree with, an ✘ next to quotes they strongly disagree with, and ignore any in between. Have the guys share their ✔'s and ✘'s, and ask them why.

Select Something to Study: Did You Know?, Get Yourself a Teacher, and/or Learn

For "Did You Know?" and "Get Yourself a Teacher," see the relevant questions under "Planning a Lesson."

Learn

 ### A List of *Mitzvot* and Customs from the Torah and Jewish Tradition

☆ What on the list is most important to you? Least important? Why?

Teacher's tip: Usually students identify ethics as most important, and activities that are seen as mostly ritual, such as *kashrut* and *t'filah*, as least important. Point out that often rituals remind us of ethics.

> ✡ What commandments and customs do you think are the minimum for you to feel that you have a Jewish identity?

Teacher's tip: This will vary from student to student.

> ✡ What commandments and customs do you think are the minimum to ensure a Jewish future?

Teacher's tip: This will also vary from student to student. Explore the differences, if any, between what is right for them versus what is right for the survival of the Jewish people. If they believe it is important for the survival of the Jewish people, is it okay for them not to do it but expect someone else to do so?

 ## Moses Maimonides: The Middle Path

> ✡ What is Maimonides trying to teach about a life of healthy emotional balance? How does this impact trying to be the kind of person you want to be?

Teacher's tip: Maimonides is trying to point out the danger of going to extremes. He is saying that being healthy means not getting carried away in any direction.

> ✡ What are some ways you think you can go to extremes? What is the result?

Teacher's tip: Students can identify times when they have lost their tempers, were impatient, or were too boastful, for example.

> ✡ Are there times when being extreme for something is a good thing? How or when?

Teacher's tip: Sometimes pushing the limits is a good thing. Standing up for yourself or someone else means not backing down, and most of the people who have made history were willing to get into trouble.

Who Is an Ideal Man?

☆ Who in your life represents wisdom?

Teacher's tip: Suggest grandparents, parents, and teachers.

☆ Strength?

Teacher's tip: Suggest something different from physical strength but strength of character.

☆ Wealth?

Teacher's tip: Suggest someone who does not have a lot of money but is happy.

☆ Social respect?

Teacher's tip: Suggest someone who is not famous but is quietly respected by his or her peers and depended upon.

☆ How would you define "success"?

Teacher's tip: The point of this exercise is to redefine success beyond fame, money, and power. Instead, being willing to learn, to have self-control and character, to learn to be content, and to respect others are also forms of success.

Journaling Time: What Do I Think?

Give students quiet time to journal in the spaces provided in the book. If you are doing this with a group, remind them you will be reading these journals privately, and you will not share anything that is written with the group. Respect privacy.

Close the Lesson: Text Connection and Possible Activity

Choose one of the options explained under "Planning a Lesson."

Notes

1. Sylvia Barack Fishman and Daniel Parmer, "Matrilineal Ascent/Patrilineal Descent: The Gender Imbalance in American Jewish Life," Hadassah-Brandeis Institute, Maurice & Marilyn Cohen Center for Modern Jewish Studies (CMJS). 2008: 1, 75. www.bjpa.org/Publications/details.cfm?PublicationID=931.

2. Fishman and Parmer, 75.

3. Fishman and Parmer, 4.

4. Fishman and Parmer, 76, 77.

Additional Resources

For Jewish Teenage Guys

Feinstein, Edward. *Tough Questions Jews Ask: A Young Adult's Guide to Building a Jewish Life,* 2nd ed. Woodstock, VT: Jewish Lights Publishing, 2011.

Mack, Stan. *The Story of the Jews: a 4,000-Year Adventure—a Graphic History Book.* Woodstock VT: Jewish Lights Publishing, 2001.

Guy Oseary, Ben Stiller, and Perry Farrell, *Jews Who Rock.* New York: St. Martin's Press, 2001.

Pearl, Judea and Ruth, eds. *I Am Jewish: Personal Reflections Inspired by the Last Words of Daniel Pearl.* Woodstock VT: Jewish Lights Publishing, 2005.

Salkin, Jeffrey K. *For Kids—Putting God on Your Guest List: How to Claim the Spiritual Meaning of Your Bar or Bat Mitzvah,* 2nd ed. Woodstock VT: Jewish Lights Publishing, 2007.

———, ed. *Text Messages: A Torah Commentary for Teens.* Woodstock, VT: Jewish Lights Publishing, 2012.

Sheinkin, Steve. *The Adventures of Rabbi Harvey: A Graphic Novel of Jewish Wisdom and Wit in the Wild West.* Woodstock, VT: Jewish Lights Publishing, 2006.

———. *Rabbi Harvey Rides Again: A Graphic Novel of Jewish Folktales Let Loose in the Wild West.* Woodstock, VT: Jewish Lights Publishing, 2008.

———. *Rabbi Harvey vs. the Wisdom Kid: A Graphic Novel of Dueling Jewish Folktales in the Wild West.* Woodstock, VT: Jewish Lights Publishing, 2010.

Slater, Robert. *Great Jews in Sports.* New York: Jonathan David Publishers, 2005.

Suneby, Liz, and Diane Heiman. *The Mitzvah Project Book: Making Mitzvah Part of Your Bar/Bat Mitzvah and Your Life.* Woodstock, VT: Jewish Lights Publishing, 2011.

Wolfson, Ron. *God's To-Do List: 103 Ways to Be an Angel and Do God's Work on Earth.* Woodstock VT: Jewish Lights Publishing, 2006.

Curricula for Jewish Spiritual Development and Boys

Shevet Achim: The Brotherhood, Moving Traditions, http://movingtraditions.org/programs/shevet-achim-the-brotherhood/

Ayeka: The Ayeka Package for High Schools, www.ayeka.org.il/the-ayeka-package-for/high-schools/

For Adults Interested in Learning More about Jewish Teenage Guys and Men

Boteach, Shmuley. *The Broken American Male and How to Fix Him.* New York: St. Martin's Press, 2008.

Brod, Harry, ed. *A Mensch Among Men: Explorations in Jewish Masculinity*. Freedom, CA: The Crossing Press, 1988.

Delsohn, Steve. *500 Great Things about Being a Dad*. Kansas City: Andrew McMeel Publishing, 2001.

Diamant, Anita, with Karen Kushner. *How To Be A Jewish Parent*. New York: Schocken Books, 2000.

Faber, Adele, and Elaine Mazlish. *How To Talk So Kids Will Listen & Listen So Kids Will Talk*. New York: Avon Books, 1980.

Fuchs-Kreimer, Nancy. *Parenting As a Spiritual Journey: Deepening Ordinary and Extraordinary Events into Sacred Occasions*. Woodstock, VT: Jewish Lights Publishing, 2002.

Gilbert, Roberta. *Connecting with Our Children: Guiding Principles for Parents in a Troubled World*. New York: John Wiley & Sons, 1999.

Grishaver, Joel Lurie. *The Bonding of Isaac: Stories and Essays About Gender and Jewish Spirituality*. Los Angeles: Alef Design Group, 1997.

Kindlon, Dan, and Michael Thompson. *Raising Cain: Protecting the Emotional Life of Boys*. New York: Ballantine, 2000.

Meeker, Meg. *Boys Should Be Boys: 7 Secrets to Raising Healthy Sons*. New York: Ballantine Books, 2009.

Meszler, Joseph. *A Man's Responsibility: A Jewish Guide to Being a Son, a Partner in Marriage, a Father, and a Community Leader*. Woodstock, VT: Jewish Lights Publishing, 2008.

Mogel, Wendy. *The Blessing of a B Minus* (New York: Scribner, 2010).

Olitzky, Kerry M., and Stuart M. Matlins, eds. *Jewish Men Pray: Words of Yearning, Praise, Petition, Gratitude and Wonder from Traditional and Contemporary Sources*. Woodstock, VT: Jewish Lights Publishing, 2013.

Osherson, Samuel. *Finding Our Fathers: How a Man's Life Is Shaped by His Relationship with His Father*. Chicago: Contemporary Books, 1986.

Perlstein, Linda. *Not Much Just Chillin': The Hidden Lives of Middle Schoolers*. New York: Random House, 2003.

Sachs, Brad E. *The Good Enough Teen: Raising Adolescents with Love and Acceptance (Despite How Impossible They Can Be)*. New York: HarperCollins, 2005.

Salkin, Jeffrey K. *Searching for My Brothers: Jewish Men in a Gentile World*. New York: Putnam, 1999.

____, ed. *The Modern Men's Torah Commentary: New Insights from Jewish Men on the 54 Weekly Torah Portions*. Woodstock, VT: Jewish Lights Publishing, 2009.

Shaffer, Susan Morris, and Linda Perlman Gordon. *Why Boys Don't Talk and Why We Care*. Chevy Chase, MD: Mid-Atlantic Equity Consortium, 2000.

About the authors of *The JGuy's Guide: A GPS for Jewish Teen Guys*

Rabbi Joseph B. Meszler is a noted spiritual leader and educator, recognized for his ability to connect the importance of Jewish tradition with everyday life. He is author of *A Man's Responsibility: A Jewish Guide to Being a Son, a Partner in Marriage, a Father and a Community Leader* and *Witnesses to the One: The Spiritual History of the* Sh'ma (both Jewish Lights). He is the rabbi at Temple Sinai in Sharon, Massachusetts, and an instructor at the Kehillah Schechter Academy.

Dr. Shulamit Reinharz is the Potofsky Professor of Sociology at Brandeis University, where she serves as founding director of both the Hadassah-Brandeis Institute and the Women's Studies Research Center. She is co-author of *The JGirl's Guide: The Young Jewish Woman's Handbook for Coming of Age* (Jewish Lights)

Liz Suneby and **Diane Heiman** are co-authors of *The Mitzvah Project Book: Making Mitzvah Part of Your Bar/Bat Mitzvah ... and Your Life* and *It's a ... It's a ... It's a Mitzvah* (both Jewish Lights).

Praise for *The JGuy's Guide*

"I often tell the story about how my life has been a journey and, had I turned left instead of right, who knows where I may have ended up. [This] book gives you that perspective about making choices in life."

—**Andre Tippett**, member of the Pro Football Hall of Fame and National Jewish Sports Hall of Fame

"Chock full of Jewish and peer wisdom on the things that teen boys think about. What a gift!"

—**Rabbi Sid Schwarz**, senior fellow, Clal; founder, Panim Institute for Jewish Leadership and Values; author, *Jewish Megatrends: Charting the Course of the American Jewish Community*

"A superb resource for working with adolescent boys. Raises timely questions, provides context for the big ideas in the book, and includes interesting material from popular culture that will engage boys."

—**Matt King**, head of Rashi School, Dedham, Massachusetts

For People of All Faiths, All Backgrounds

JEWISH LIGHTS Publishing

www.jewishlights.com

 Find us on Facebook®
Facebook is a registered
trademark of Facebook, Inc.

Printed in the USA
CPSIA information can be obtained
at www.ICGtesting.com
JSHW060048150824
68134JS00031B/2675